In the Beginning God
Created the Earth...

the Sea

The Bible Tells Me So Press

In the Beginning God Created the Earth...
the Sea

A children's book produced by
The Bible Tells Me So Press

PUBLISHED BY
THE BIBLE TELLS ME SO CORPORATION
WWW.THEBIBLETELLSMESO.COM

First Edition, November 2021

When God created the earth, He also created

water...

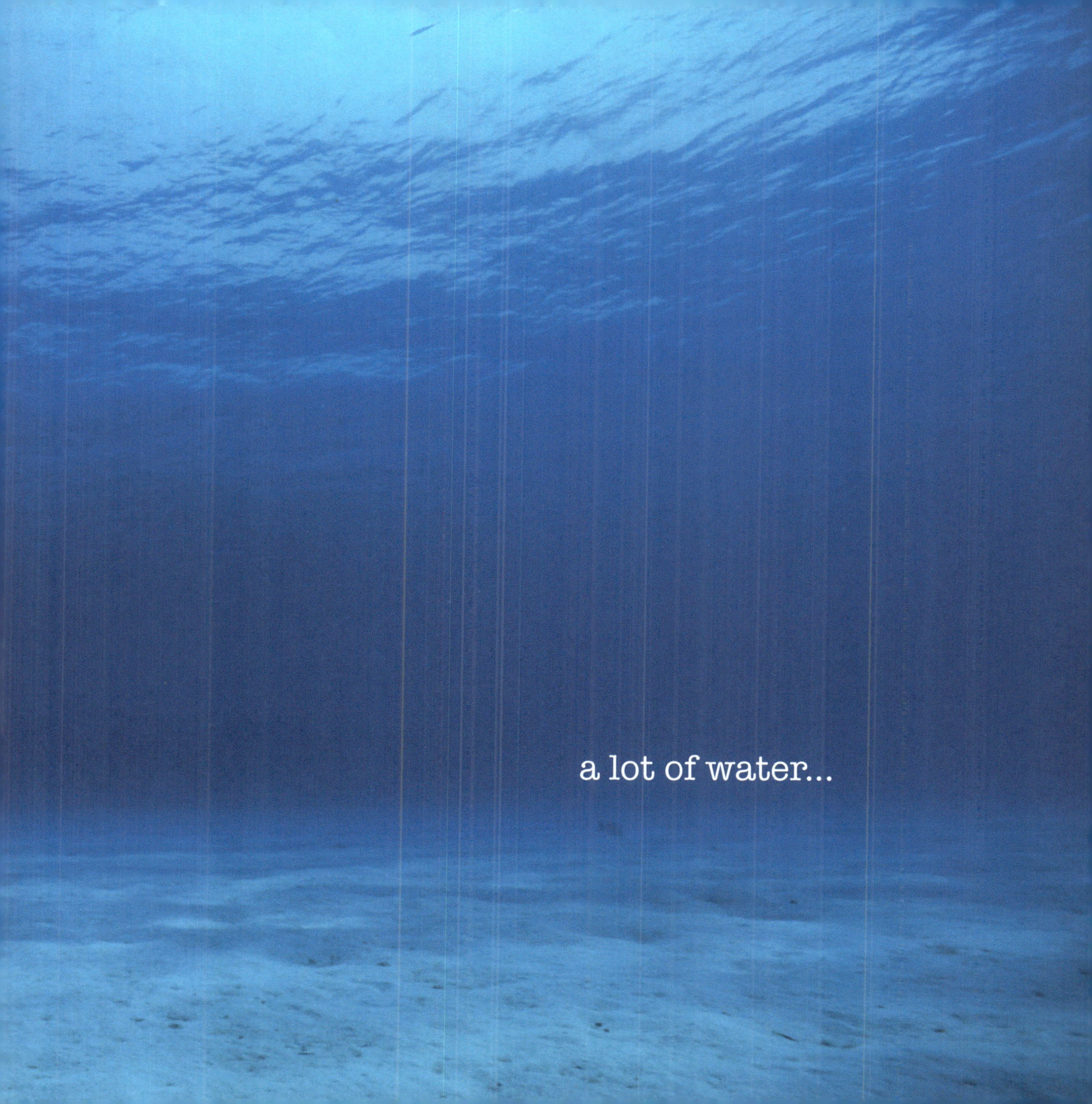

a lot of water...

over 325,000,000,000,000 gallons of water!

All
that water
covers a
whopping 71%
of the surface
of the earth.

And almost all of it
is stored in our
special,
important,
and incredible
sea.

Earth

Venus

Earth

Mars

Earth

Mercury

The sea is special,
and it makes the earth
a very special place as well.
No other planet compares
to the earth with its
amazing sea.

(Planets are not shown to scale.)

Earth  Jupiter
(a gas planet)

Saturn
(a gas planet)

Earth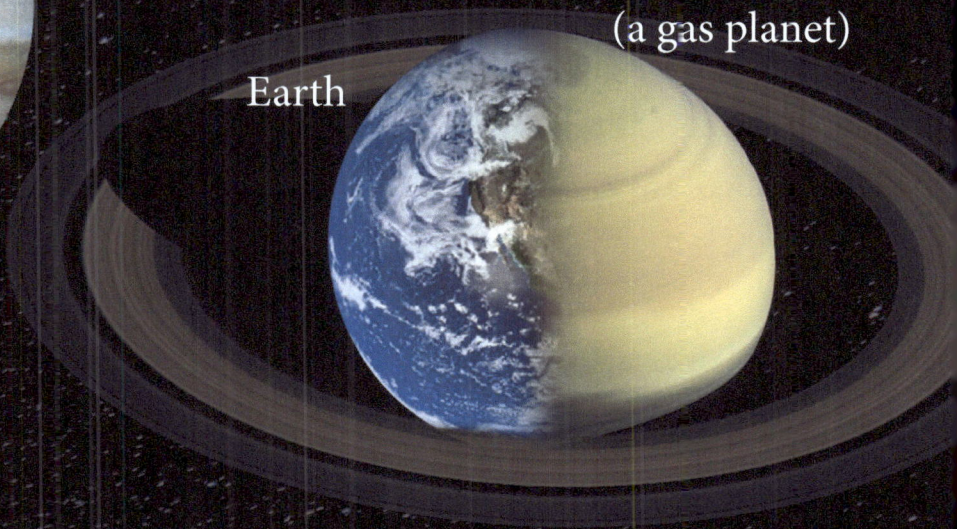

This could never
have happened
by chance.

Earth

Earth

Neptune
(a gas planet)

Uranus
(a gas planet)

But the sea
is not only special,
it's also very
important, because
without all that
water it would be
impossible for us
to live.

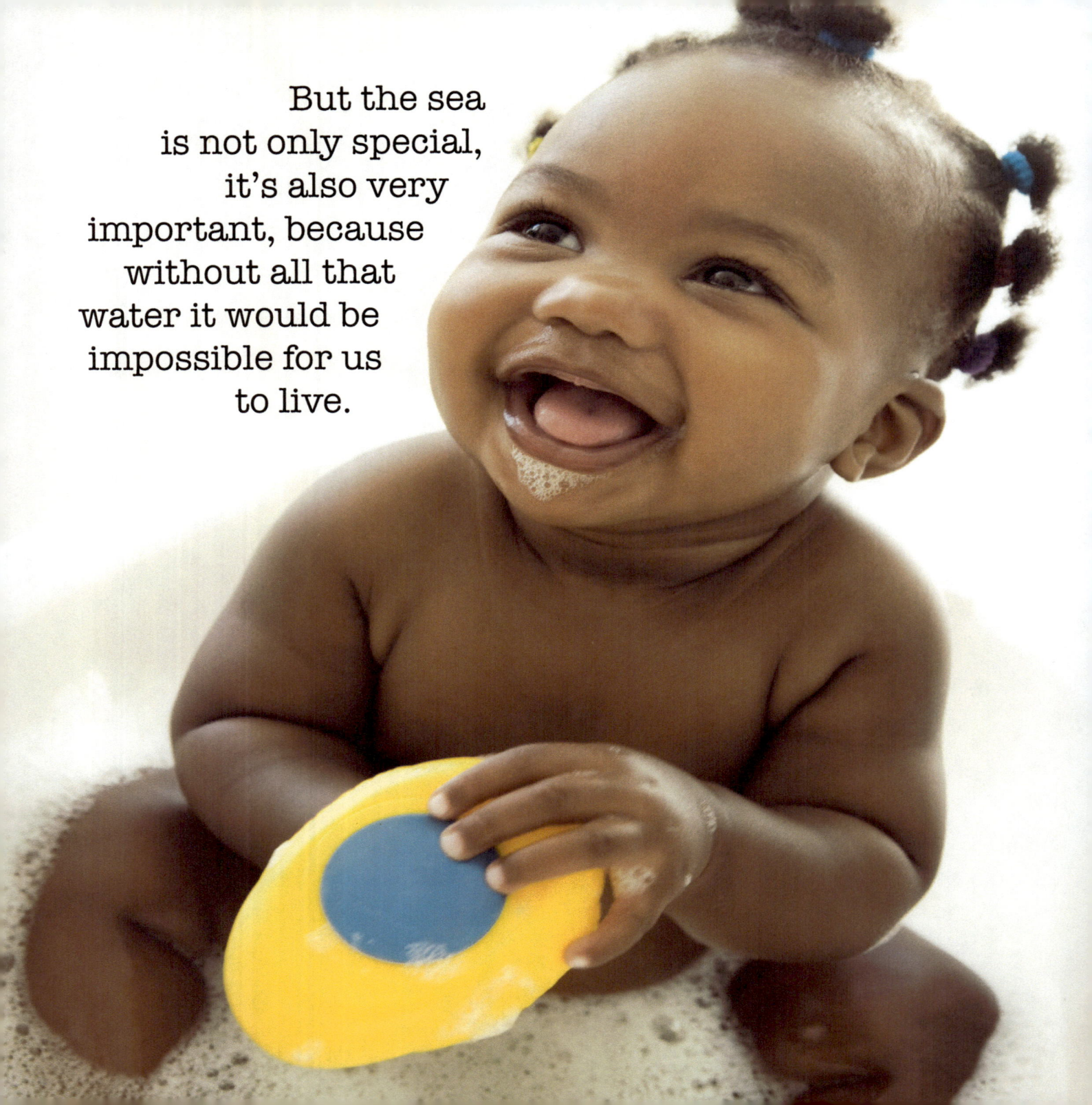

In fact, our bodies
are mostly
made up
of water.

The sea
is also important because,
along with the trees, it produces the oxygen
that we need. It helps to filter out harmful
things in the air,

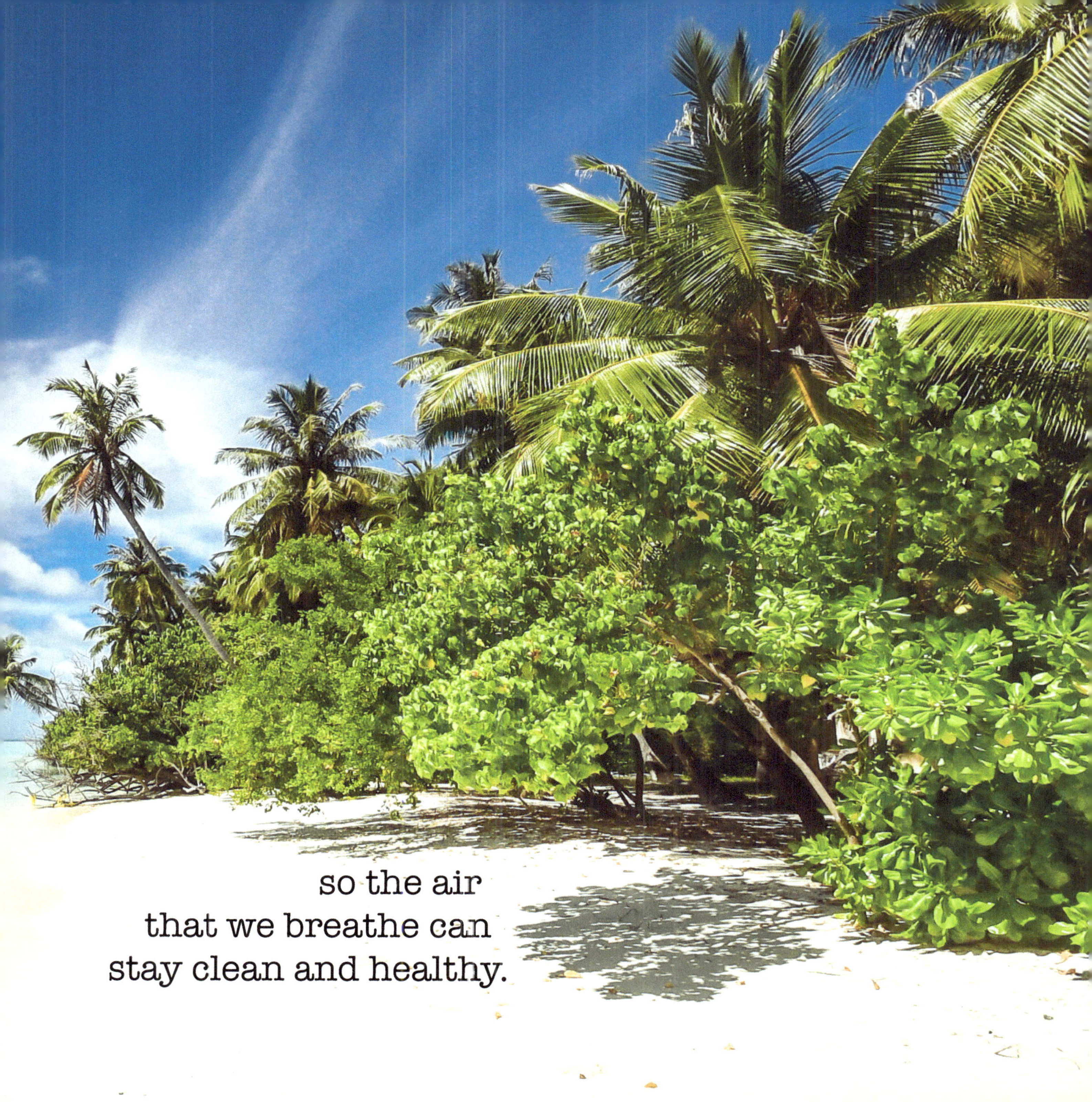

so the air
that we breathe can
stay clean and healthy.

And it absorbs heat from the sun
to keep the earth's temperature within
a perfect range for us to live.

It's like a giant thermostat
to keep us safe and comfortable
all the time.

But the sea is not only special and important,

it's also incredible

because
it provides
a home for
over 3 trillion fish
and other animals
to live in.

Some sea animals, like this
humpback whale and her calf,

are really big!

While others, like this little clownfish
hiding in a sea anemone,

are very small.

The sea
is an incredible source of food
for millions of people
around the world.

And the sea
is incredible
in ways that we still
haven't discovered.

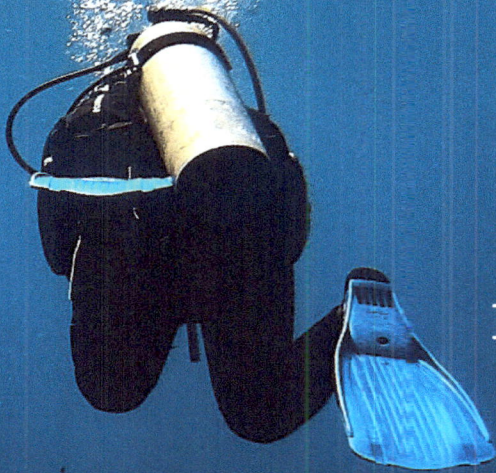

Because
the sea is so big,
we've haven't even
explored 5% of it!

Yes,
the sea
that God
created for us
is special,
important,
and incredible.

It's just what we need.

So, the next time
you swim at the beach,
drive along the coast,
or ride in a boat,

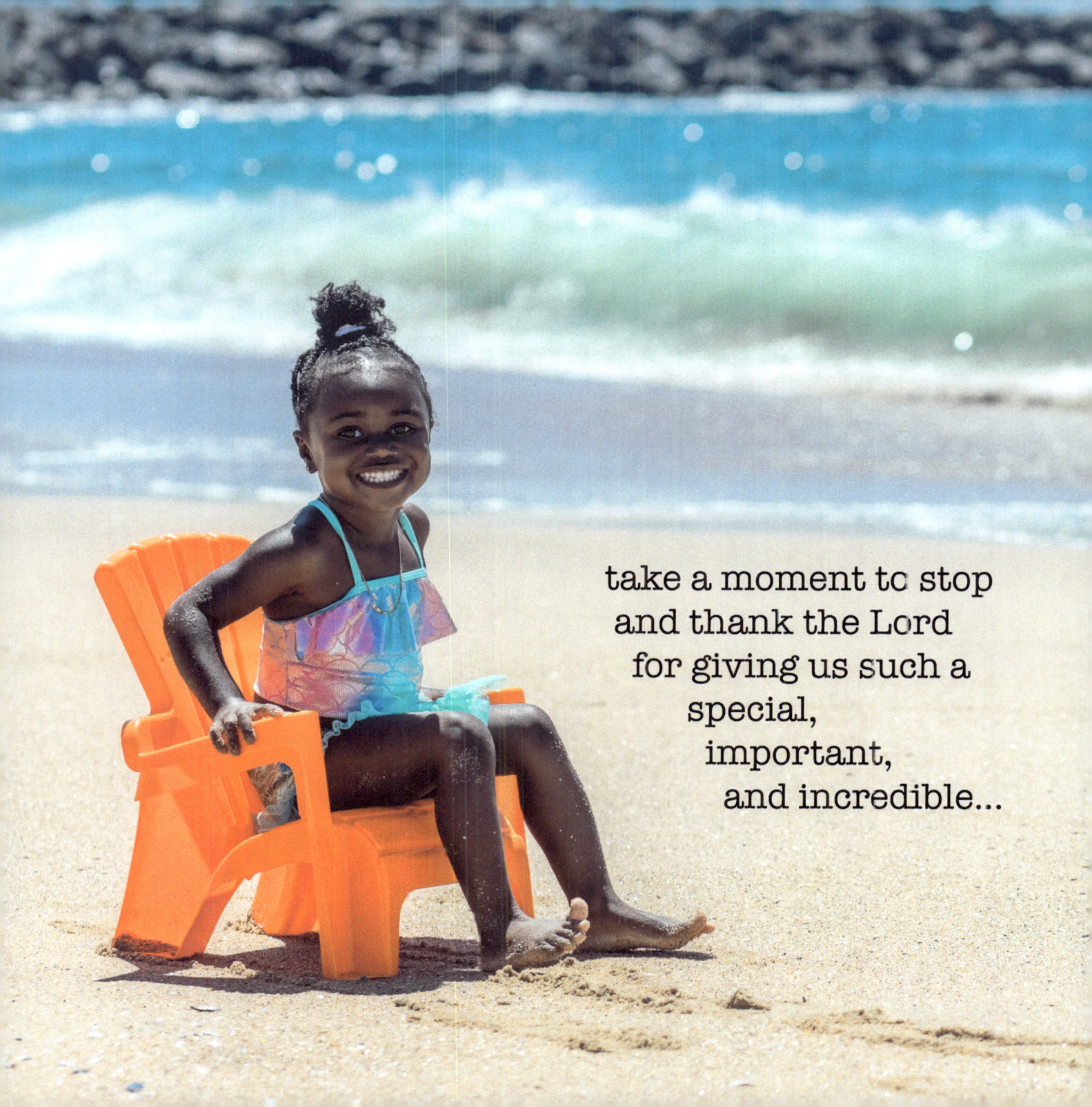

take a moment to stop
and thank the Lord
for giving us such a
special,
important,
and incredible...

sea.

The sea is His,
and He made it.

Psalm 95:5a

For more
books, videos, songs, and crafts,
visit us online at
TheBibleTellsMeSo.com

™

The Bible
Tells Me
So.com

Standing on the Bible and growing!